Self-Control: A Mind Game or A Heart Game?

Several stories that question if you are a slave or a master of Your thinking processes

DAVID MUGUN

Published by The Scribe Centre

P.O. Box 35 – 00621

Nairobi, Kenya.

Contents

DEDICATION

To all the business people who leave nothing to chance.

ACKNOWLEDGEMENTS

To Almighty God for seeing me through yet another book project.

To everyone who has been a positive influencer in my life.

Chapter 1

Snippets Of How They Control You In, Or, As A Crowd

It all depends on what comprises your universe. Is it a family, a WhatsApp group, an organisation with hundreds of employees; a country, or the whole world? Your universe best dictates the most suitable resources, tactics and strategies. Tactics are short term in nature while strategies are long-term based. Control is about wielding power over others.

Let us begin with relationships between a man and a woman. Humans have an emotional side represented by reasoning from the heart. They also have a rational side represented by reasoning from the mind. When the two work simultaneously, they meet midway and help to maintain a healthy balance as the relationship has rationalised emotions.

When we keep to either extreme with men digging into the rational side and the women firmly anchored on the emotional end or vice versa, it takes the delicate application of skills to return to normalcy and this is where the rational mind is manipulated using well-reasoned arguments and seasoned with just enough emotion.

The emotional type is tugged in using heart seeking talks and actions. To sustain the relationship, either partner takes into consideration the building blocks which include: a long-term side, something to look forward to at all times, a shared culture, finances, common interests and a supportive attitude. These are also the tools of control.

Let us not get into the nitty-gritty. Everyone knows their mate well enough to exercise control over them. The pants' wearer keeps shifting between the couple depending on their relationship's emotion/reason dynamics. For the traditionalist, other rules apply.

At the family level, there are as many manipulative styles as there are families. Different styles work with different age groups and the simplest form is continuous crying by a child or by one of the parents. The most effective styles depend on family culture.

 Some parents exercise power simply by just clearing their throats, and immediately, the children know that it is bedtime even if their favourite program was airing on TV. A second clearing of the throat spells doom for the defiant child.

 Some parents make everyone around them feel guilty to firmly maintain control while others make kids do things that get them to continuously search for perfection. Many set unattainable targets to escape financial obligations.

Some get their kids to feel like heroes all the time. But the true test of the success of this approach manifests when the kids are up against giants and minions. Will they be consistent or do they collapse?

Different approaches bring different results.

In WhatsApp groups, the admin is meant to be fully in charge but we have many invited characters who do different things to shape the opinions of members around the prevailing discussions.

Liberal admins leave the groups to find their own flow but five characters are constant and will always control our discussions.

First, is the admin who controls those joining or those forced to leave. They hold the disciplinary keys.

Second, are the serious guys. They want to be associated with serious discussions. Sometimes they are dismissive of those who try to lighten the moments with funny stuff. They discuss the economy, politics, and react to news items about organisations. They control the group's long-term outlook.

Third, are the jokers. They have nothing serious to say but they always comment on all topics in the group. They have all manner of things queued up in your WhatsApp chats. They don't control much but must keep sending stuff to catch everyone's attention. They test and control your patience if you allow them.

Fourth, we have the controversial guys. They twist things around. Rabble-rousers influence how people engage. Many members first watch out for what they are up to before reacting to their contributions. These guys control your reactions through irritation.

Finally, you have the guys who take care of the group's optical nutrition requirements. These guys share very catchy pictorials and videos. They are the best at filtering stuff so that the most impactful make it in the forum. Many times, all who subscribes to their contribution look forward to their juicy input. They control your imagination as they keep you yearning for more.

Let's focus on the workplace. Organisations have people wishing to control them for whatever reasons those people have.

Effective bosses know something about everyone and will attempt to utilise everyone for something other than their work. Some people are good at arranging parties and meetings and others are good at spotting business opportunities. Whatever it is, the bosses try to use them positively or suppress them depending on how it benefits them or the organisation. They control the opportunities that come your way or are kept from you.

Two main types of employees also bring out two kinds of bosses. First, we have employees who understand that the boss must never be challenged for power in any way when opportunities to do so present themselves. They do a good job and await to be pulled up the ranks for they are no threat.

This type of employees usually rises faster because the bosses want to have a dependable guy who isn't a threat even after they exit the organisation. And many times, it's for personal gain. These types work like good conductors of electricity by never disrupting the flow of control.

Then we have another type. This is the guy with plenty of self-belief. They have all the required competencies and have an attitude of challenging and questioning the system. They push their way up unlike the first type that gets pulled up. They work like a self-regulated cut-out switch and can disrupt the flow of power and control.

So, these two kinds of employees thrive under different types of bosses. 90% of the time, bosses wish for those who can be pulled up. This type of boss and junior pair up well in status quo dependent situations such as where longevity is driven by shared secrets like hidden deals. When hard times manifest through economic or pandemic challenges, the first type of bosses clings on to anything else that maintains familiarity. This includes the predictable employee types.

Unfortunately for them, desperate times call for the self-driven types and dynamic bosses acknowledge this attribute as a vital contributor to the organisation's success. Smart bosses send these types to head branches away from the headquarters. These guys will get things done with limited supervision. So, the dynamic boss will exercise control by utilising every employee in the place where their positive impact is felt the most.

At the country level, we know that not everyone is of the same circumstances in terms of knowledge levels, wealth, gender, affiliations et al, all the time. Every government exists to uplift and grow the aspirations, living standards and to ensure the security of its citizenry. But no government is in full control of all the circumstances within its jurisdiction.

So, they are forced to be creative with control strategies and tactics. Most times, they go along what citizens like. For instance, sport is a big area for crowd control. All sporting activities have fans and their favourite teams form a big part of their conversations and priorities.

There have been instances in other countries where mass action was contained by threats to cancel football matches because of the potential friction between the authorities and the fans. For the ardent fan, the stadium experience cannot be traded for any other option and this has worked. But perhaps not in situations where the reasons for mass action rank higher than the upcoming game.

In other countries, widely practised activities are utilised by the authorities as control baits. For as long as these activities are tied to long term gains, and that they keep reasonably high levels of hope, the masses bite hard.

Maize farming is one such activity here at home. It occupies many people. We know that everyone else in the supply chain of inputs is the true gainer. Even better for you if you are an importer. At the end of it all, the hope for a different result annually, keeps the millions of people dependent on maize growing, focussed and occupied by the cereal's politics. They are disappointed but the allure of next year's fortunes soon takes over. And the government ticks off the box of yet another year of crowd control success as it kept the peace.

Price discrimination is another favourite tool. Water finds its own level. We all fall into place based on what we can afford. To keep people away from certain areas, you either secure them using the police, watchmen, technology-based measures or you simply use pricing. If it has a scarcity element to it, the better.

When people vote with their pockets, the majority find themselves in densely populated neighbourhoods as the monied families' breath the fresh air provided by their leafy surroundings.

Aspiration for a better life is in itself a control measure that plays out throughout our lives. That is why every government must cultivate and maintain the hopes of its citizens. There is nothing worse for authorities than fighting to control a multitude that has lost hope. They have nothing to lose anymore and they now direct their energy to any course that exacts revenge for slipping into hopelessness.

At the world stage, muscle wins you, friends. The rich and powerful countries dictate the pace for mankind. They decide for the world. The formal structures at the global stage work for them and when they want to discuss things that matter to them alone, they go offline and use an informal gathering called the

G7. The ramifications of this informal club, find their way into the formal workings of many lesser governments.

In geopolitics, some amended principles of physics apply. For instance, "for every action, there is an equal and opposite reaction." The difference here is that the G7 determines both the actions and the reactions.

For their countries to continue thriving, the opposite must happen in some poor African country. To grow their technological dominance, they must create a banana republic to supply the critical raw materials that feed their tech-based companies. They then come back to give grants and loans from the proceeds. They instigate and control the undemocratic events at the source countries whilst exercising democratic principles at home.

Further, they come for the continent's best brains and make these brains work for them throughout their productive lives. The spent forces then return with accents and stories.

This article is not exhaustive but it nonetheless serves to stimulate further discussions.

As an individual, what do you control? That is your admission ticket to bigger things to control, for, at any stage, practice makes perfect for the next big thing.

Chapter 2

It takes For An Innovator To Be Known At Home

Let us think from a brand perspective.

We often hear that a prophet is never known at home. They make their name far away and let the emotions stirred by the unexpected fame lead to acceptance or jealousy in equal measure.

We also hear that charity begins at home but often, good deeds at home are mistaken for political moves or other unintended motives.

Albert Einstein, the most famous scientist of his time, was not known or celebrated at home in the German empire until his works, during the cold war era, filtered through to a professor in the west. And while visiting the USA in 1933, Hitler came to power. Given Einstein's Jewish roots, there was no turning back thereafter because he relocated completely so that he could harness the opportunities freely available to him in the west.

We often use one's past and known present time to judge them. This becomes a permanent mental screen of that person and we stubbornly stick to it no matter what. This is the dilemma that a senior person encounters when a junior overtakes him in the chain of command at work. He will not readily accept the new fact.

The same afflicts those from privileged backgrounds when a poor kid does better than them in life. They prefer to judge him based on his past and not the present or future.

For many people, the fear of the spotlight for good deeds tethers them to a life dictated by lesser brains. It is far much easier to discourage than to encourage someone.

People are also a lot more comfortable with temporary situations such as the presence of a foreigner at work or college because they won't compete with them in the long term. They are far removed from domestic fights and on a compounding basis, they tend to do better than the locals as they are very alert about their foreign status. They will therefore make hay as the sun shines.

Back at his home in the USA, Napoleon Hill was a certified failure. His life was littered with everything that could possibly go wrong in a man's life. Yet in the midst of all this, Andrew Carnegie, a successful man, challenged him to research and document his findings in a book on how to succeed. His book: "Think And Grow Rich" was the result of interviewing several successful people at the time. The book has made it to the top ten bestselling self-help books of all time.

Napoleon Hill went on to become a success because Andrew Carnegie saw the prophet in him at home. It took a man far removed from the pettiness of the masses to identify the next big thing literally from the most obvious failure. If this does not happen frequently in your environment, then know that even those you think are successful around you, are nothing more than monied but negative spirits. Their fruits should be plain for all to see. Genuinely successful people aid deserving people to harness their full potential.

95% of the time, you will come across a negative spirit. All you need initially is to spend 95% of your time searching for that good spirit within the 5% of genuine types. The process of knowing one more person to avoid is just as important as finding that one person that will make the difference in you. Trees denied of the blowing winds that bend them back and forth as they grow, often fall to the ground when fully grown. This is because what stresses them as they grow, hardens them for their own good.

So, what happens when a prophet is known at home? Or the question ought to be: How does one become a prophet at home?

A prophet is widely declared so because they are famous. But it all begins somewhere. There is always that one person that gets you into the limelight. That one person that mainstreams you. We need to focus more on these people that launch prophets from a brand perspective.

Success bequeaths success. The good spirits that have walked the success path, normally go full circle and handhold a deserving spirit along this path less trodden.

The one getting supported will have demonstrated promise and the guide knows from where to progress matters moving forward. What we need more, is the ability to tell the genuine role models from the fakes. Genuine types have no jealousy or funny tricks. They are not users out to profit from novices.

If you are willing to submit to their apprenticeship, then you are on the right path to being a prophet at home. The genuine guys don't judge you by your present or past but by your potential. They are often busy and know who can be just as productively busy as they are.

For the prophet in the making, crucial skills are needed in understanding how to approach and sustain a productive relationship with successful types. Never start on a wrong footing. Even the educated fail because they are not schooled. Get tips from one who has gone down that road.

To make it at home, it is prudent to take your time to spot genuinely successful types. When they support you, then the real meaning of "charity begins at home" comes to pass. This year, be the positive spirit that will hold and guide a deserving spirit.

Chapter 3

Why A Template-Based Mentality Can Make Or Break Us

The routines that have engulfed our lives and dictated our modus operandi largely contribute the reasons why we succeed or fail in equal measure. We must always bear in mind that different protocols serve well under specific conditions. It is always a change in routine that gives us away when working incognito. Similarly, it is always the change in prevailing conditions that render certain routines ineffective.

Often, we go to our favourite restaurant for a cup of tea because they make it better than all the others. But is this true?

The one thing that remains constant for most people is the "two spoons of sugar" practice. I discovered that the tea at my favourite restaurant tasted much sweeter because they use a relatively smaller-sized cup yet my two spoons of sugar preference goes on unabated.

Psychologically, because the tea is served in a pot, and I get three cups, I feel that it is value-for-money both quantitatively and qualitatively, but it is a trick that has worked since the first home dining room became a restaurant.

My other preferred restaurant is a good rendezvous for business meetings and their tea doesn't taste as good as that at my favourite restaurant simply because they use bigger cups which dilute my two spoons of sugar to a near plain taste.

If I can mentally prepare for the extra sugar needed in the bigger cup - health parameters allowing, I might just upgrade this restaurant above my present favourite.

We are creatures of habit and our inability to make suitable adjustments denied us by deeply lodged templates, only ensures that we return actions consistent with the instructions inscribed therein.

Some find it easy to adjust but the majority find solace in familiar routines.

When scouts or members of the disciplined forces are forward-matching as a team and one person is out of step despite the instructions given, the leader can either stop the whole group or shout out the name of the odd one out of step and ask him to "change step". From then on, the matching proceeds in perfect unison.

Many of us need to change step upon observing that there exists a variance between our normal routines and those demanded by the new environment.

The last year has been a time of disrupted routines. Physical movement has had new protocols imposed by respective authorities. For some, the rules in place make no sense and their failure to adjust has come out as defiance.

Despite the obvious flows that arise from our routine guided approaches, we are better off having them than playing in an unguided state. Safety procedures in any discipline are crucial for our comfort and survival.

Sports such as golf, depend on strict adherence to specific routines for a player to remain successful.

But in general life, we know that variety is the spice of life. To please someone, we go out of the ordinary to make that difference that scores us the points. But even in doing so, we employ a routine that we hardly use to get us the results needed at that moment.

So, it's time that we do a self-review and consider every routine, step by step. We must debug them so that they are fit for purpose.

Now I look at the size of the cup to determine how much sugar to add to my tea.

Routines bring order to our lives but we must let them serve and not enslave us.

Chapter 4

The Consequences Of Oscillating Between The Stone
Age and The Information Age

Give a 6-year old child an old cell phone - of the *mulika* series
and he will play with it as a toy. But give him a smartphone and
he will immediately know what to do with it. Similarly, get a
millennial kid behind a manual vehicle and they will be clueless
but behind an automatic transmission vehicle, they are like fish
thrown into the water, they swim effortlessly.

Those are just two examples of relatively modern times that
epitomize the discomforting nature of out-of-date contraptions.

The irony of life is such that the more we advance
technologically, the more likely it is for us to lapse back to the
previous stages, and all in an instant.

It is now official that there has been more information
developed and shared globally over the past two years than

previously and going backwards to creation. Thanks to information technology.

In the stone age, a solar eclipse and the overwhelming effects of alcohol were the only known blackouts. Today, in an electricity-dependent world, blackouts momentarily return us to stone age times. Without electricity, we cannot access information, use our home appliances and much more. We lose our competitive edge and more importantly, the speed necessary to cope in today's world.

There are just four ages - Stone age, Agrarian, Industrial and the Information age.

The stone age was dominated by hunter-gatherers. Bows and arrows brought success.

The agrarian age had the hoe as the tool of success, later, mechanisation took over.

The industrial age had machines that required a huge labour force to keep the factories running.

Today, much as the information age has made nonsense of all earlier advancements, it has failed in one thing. It has not yet given us a full-proof exit from the earlier ages.

A power outage momentarily takes us back to all or either of the earlier forms of life. We often rely on the aphorism that: "not knowing something off head is of less importance than knowing where you can find the information when you need it". The power outage that I experienced in the middle of an urgent assignment recently, completely destroyed any truth in this school of thought because I could not access the internet when I needed to.

Every age requires a totally different set of skills to survive. Too many changes from forced oscillations require the use of more time, money and energy to compensate for the anomalies. This is why you buy a generator even if you are connected to the grid because you know better. Unfortunately, the generator set takes you back several thousand or millions of shillings because of the inherent failures to prompt service and make timely replacements in a rickety power grid.

The same goes for health insurance which is big business and the salient reminder of a failed public system despite taxes getting paid. Denial of access to health facilities on account of lacking medical cover condemns one to pre-independence options that are still available at a fee.

Bad roads remind us often that the technology in the contraptions that we drive never had such roads in mind. They were designed for the conditions in those countries that make them. What we do here is improvisation.

A life filled with improvisations is one of toil on account of the kind of failure that got the president to admit that Kes. 2 billion is stolen from our coffers daily.

Every leader that steals your money is the exemplification of a winch that steadily pulls you backwards into stone age times. What is meant to lead you away from backwardness keeps you right there so that they alone enjoy the fruits of the information age.

Now our oscillations between the stone age and the information age are aided by our choices between good, disguised as bad and bad, disguised as good. Even the most intelligent fall prey to the choices made at the ballot.

So, stone-age leadership only brings us a stone-age lifestyle. Every stage has its effective leadership style. If your boss treats you like a farmhand, then his style is best suited for the times gone by in the agrarian age. You don't have to behave like an industrial age native to prove your industriousness, we have new metrics to guide us on that today.

Chapter 5

When It Pays To Forget - Corporate Institutional
Memory Is On Trial

A man awoke from a 15-year coma and regained his memory in
an astonishingly short period of one month. But this wasn't the
case for the inactive muscles during the period as physiotherapy
took a much longer time to ignite his motor skills.

He was chauffeured on his maiden trip around the city by his
20-year old son, who was a little 5-year old at the time of the
accident that sent him into comatose. It was in a strange-
looking car because the one he knew was long gone and had
defrayed some of his hospitalisation costs. And so, he asked:
"Why wasn't I consulted when selling my car?" The boy was too
young at the time so he simply answered: "you were deep in
your long sleep dad and we needed to keep you alive".

The shock was evident and just as the doctor had told the
family, the freshly awoken man needed a year to get up to
speed.

Life had moved on so fast that the man had to reconcile himself with the fact that this was not a sneak preview of the future but rather a time to play catch up with all the fundamentals that now confronted him. He also needed to come to terms with a past that he never had a chance to influence.

Life itself became an oxymoron and excitingly frustrating at that for everyone around him. It sometimes turned to frustratingly exiting. Every move or thought kept reminding everyone else of a time that they had moved away from: "Let's visit the Petersons", he requested and he was updated on their formal separation a decade ago. Some people from his life then had passed away and nearly a half of his acquaintances had retired or moved away in search of success.

The digital world that faced him now was monstrous and his daily therapy began to make more sense at every session that he attended. As he fully processed events that had happened, everyone else needed to move on with their lives and it was not easy.

Today, many people are dazed by the speed of change. The last 18 months alone have churned out more information than all that was out there from the beginning of time. Technology is the enabler here. During this time, the devourer in Covid-19 arose and wreaked havoc on our lives - the possibility of a deadlier wave poses a real danger on lives and more jobs.

So, adjustments today bequeath more adjustments the way problems call their relatives to the party when one is experiencing hard times. In the interim period, we must find a coping mechanism now and a lasting solution moving forward.

Such huge changes to cope with for many people are akin to an awakening from a long coma. Suddenly, the many things that we cling to can no longer bring us success or pride. We must let go of them and embrace what the new day has in store.

When something matters for the next phase of survival, adults take learning seriously. We are now at that point where forgetting the irrelevant past only pays if we embrace the realities of today with the gusto of a child learning to speak or walk. Giving up is not an option.

Just as professionals have a minimum number of Continuous Professional Development points to achieve from new programs offered annually, if they must renew their practising certificates, we must now set our own targets along a similar path. It is not a choice but a must-do item on our list.

Panic mode must not set in. There is always a way out of any quagmire. When things look complex, give it a simple approach. So just simply ask yourself, where am I now vis-a-vis my new destination? Where you are now is what you either must forget or what cannot bring you success for the world buried it under the hip of new opportunities. And that is where you must search for your future activities.

The next question is, what do I need to do to get where I am destined? This is where you map out your way through uncharted waters and it is a frightening phase as you are confronting a reality that won't be rehearsed for things shall go live for sure. And finally, what resources do I need to get where I am headed? Hope and self-belief are some of them.

If those resources include people who are knowledgeable about your chosen path, then seek them out. Your enemy from the old world may be the best ally in your future path, he needs to survive too. So, however hard it is, forgiving without throwing caution to the wind is the best way of forgetting the past for it shall progress you to your next phase in life.

Letting go is not a talent that anyone was given. It is an order that we must obey. Today's fundamentals are calling the shots from unfamiliar grounds and none that you were told about in good time.

Institutional memory is on trial here and no wonder that some organisations are registering growth even when the old hands are terminated. In some instances, their exit at work spurs mega growth. Such are the times to disembark and write a book about the good old times. At least you will be selling it in the present tense as you ponder your next move.

The good news in the midst of these enormous shifts is that humans, unlike dinosaurs, are versatile enough to surmount the tide. Just play your part in the change process and you will remake your future.

Chapter 6

Why Is The Economy Increasingly Found In Fewer Pockets Today?

Or do we have many torn pockets in our midst?

Let us first get over with the definitions of the term "economy".

First, economy is the state of a country or region in terms of the production and consumption of goods and services and the supply of money.

Second, the economy refers to the careful management of available resources.

A third definition that resonates with the majority is that the economy refers to how financial resources flow in and out of our pockets. We have people who are today referred to as the economy in their own right. When a rich guy from the city arrives in the village for the weekend, the neighbours say that the economy has come and knowing what's best for them, they show up with requests to be handed money for this problem or the other.

So why is it that some people have money while others don't?

I will be as diverse as I can get.

We have monied people who genuinely earned what they have because of working for it. There are three ways that one can earn money in this category.

You can earn by giving your time in exchange for a fee or a salary. 90% of earners fall under this section. They can be hired or fired but while at it, they earn money.

You can also earn money by investing money to make you more money. This is when you buy shares or when you buy into a private opportunity. About 5% or so of the people with money fall under this section.

But 1% of the people fall under this final section of our first category. They make money by multiplying time. This is done through many sources of income. When you have multiple sources of income, you can make money while asleep. These are our industrialists, our professionals with multiple revenue streams.

If you are not in any of those sections, then you won't experience the economy in friendly ways.

But there is another reason why you may be finding it hard to grow your involvement in the economy. As we stand, we have both positive and negative strategies for managing market share erosion. Existing market players always find ways of attaining and then maintaining dominance. It is in these strategies that they can make more money. Let us focus on the negative strategies.

Follow this story with me.

A hard-working guy decides to import some machinery to produce some high-demand products. The machines are made by the best manufacturer in that industry. They have passed that country's export standards and certified as such.

Our entrepreneur pays for the machines and hands in the documentation for pre-shipment inspection. Surprisingly, they fail the test. The report indicates that the stuff is of substandard quality. He then orders for a part by part inspection and this yields a 90% quality report with 10% failing because the parts used to assemble the machine were of poor quality. The good news is that those parts can be sourced locally. But our entrepreneur has lost four months so far. Meanwhile, back at home, the full licensing of the products to be manufactured is subject to availing samples produced by the applicant in the absence of the machines that would produce them.

What just happened is plain for experienced people to see but hard for the innocent eye to notice.

The established boys, in this case, managed to work in cahoots with elements within pre-shipment inspection companies to frustrate the entrance of new competitors into the market place.

When other agencies within governments play with some people, they do it in clever ways that make it hard to prove that one was selected against. It could be anyone's agenda provided that there are willing givers and takers.

This example shows us that the economy can be herded like cattle into some few pockets.

And so, because of the lessons from the story, many people have resorted to making money whilst insuring their activities against the sabotaging actions of established players. These people have learned to correctly read the market risk and add the extra cost of doing business in their pricing.

This additional cost of doing business is what takes away more money from our pockets more frequently and increases the number of pockets that are locked out of the economy.

The third category of money makers or losers is that where religious followers fall prey to Ponzi-like schemes. Many people give their money to false miracle workers who claim to possess money multiplication abilities. Respectable members of our society have fallen for these open theft schemes. They always end in tears.

The fourth category is the me-too jealous types. Because Peter runs a successful business and he is from your village, that entitles you to copy him even when it is obvious that you don't have the requisite skills. Instead of letting Peter become your mentor, you become his tormentor.

When someone rears chicken, everyone else gets into the business and then end up flooding the market. With bad prices due to an oversupply, everyone loses and everyone's pocket gets empty.

We have a category of lazy people who do nothing at all despite having the ability to produce. They lack self-respect and add to the liabilities of their caring friends and relatives.

Finally, we have thieves. Those that dispossess you of your hard-earned wealth. They vary from the invisible to the violent types and are physically present or in cyberspace. Your wealth is their business and they have a ready market for stolen goods.

All the categories that explain why we have money in very few pockets point to the selfish acts of others. For them to win, someone else must lose out. Fairtrade is about a reasonable exchange of value. Selfishness is the biggest reason for having an empty pocket. Count your close associates and point out those that are not selfish. They are very few of them.

Chapter 7

How To Maintain Your Balance In A Politically Charged Atmosphere

There are times when love is in the air and everything seems perfect. But love is blind to faults and obvious biases — and any contrary views held by others can cause an end to long-held friendships in response — as a safety fuse to protect the blossoming love.

Politics plays out in much the same way as love does and so are other emotive subjects as gender and religion. We may be a lover, a brother, a boss, a parent, a member and many more roles all in one including a political supporter. There are times when our various roles conflict and tend to stick out more at the expense of the others.

A position taken may isolate your child in school for no fault of his or a job can be lost for a stand taken and all because of aligning to someone who you are not known to. But just like love is, all the other roles that we play including political leanings never leave us for interests must be affirmed or sought at all times. Yet we must maintain our balance to function well. So, we must look at politics as a part of a whole and not as an independent whole. Let us use a car to illustrate the point.

And so that you don't catch feelings this early, please know that no part of the car is of more importance than the other. Size and functions differ, but it is incomplete without any single piece.

A traditional combustion engine fitted car has thousands of parts without which the automobile won't function well or even at all.

The engine needs all the natural elements to function. Air, fuel, water and heat. The heat, air and fuel must mix in the right proportions to produce the power needed to run the engine. If water enters this mix, the engine malfunctions as the water is needed in a separate chamber of the same engine to cool it just as the engine oil separately held also lubricates the moving parts to keep the engine efficiencies at optimal levels.

The steering system plays the parental role for behind it a stable person is needed to steer it to and from planned destinations. It is never the politicians behind the wheel but if they do, the car won't get back home.

The tyres are the friends. They are necessary all the time but as their importance wears out, they get replaced.

The engine represents the total population. One nation but with people and communities playing different roles in keeping the socio-economic systems running.

If you thought that politics was the engine or even the fuel, you are wrong. The fuel represents the relatives. They light up when we are all doing well and they show up at the least expected times like flooding the plugs and misfiring the system. They are family and a source of identity nonetheless.

The shock absorbers are the religious groups. They grieve with you and solve your hard problems without complaining. Bad shocks can cause an accident or aid in the sustained damage of several parts in the car. They must always work well. When well, they make your life journey smoother.

The sensors across the entire car are the law and order system. And only available in newer or more advanced civilizations. Sometimes they act as expected and at times, they are a nuisance and especially when they are helping the bad guys. When a temperature sensor fails, it gets the car to keep sending excessive amounts of fuel into the combustion chamber and causes havoc.

So, who are the political class? They are the lighting system. The headlamps, fog lights, cabin lights and blinkers.

The headlamps, just as politicians are work best at night and are not as useful during the day, they are off in the daylight for that is our time to see for ourselves. Some work best as indicators and other work best in cold weather as the fog lights do. Some politicians are the brake lights, if they don't work, the tailing cars may knock us. They can never be the engine because they are there for a season and a reason as voted for by the engine, (the society). Politicians exist to shed light and not to shade it from us. Ladies, is it fair to liken politicians to anything in the salon? Not the blow drier, perhaps the pedicure tool for scraping off the cuticle.

So why spend more time politicking instead of checking and balancing all the other roles?

Today, as we speak, the people who demonstrate resilience in the face of harsh economic times, are those that keep politics at bay. They serve in their roles religiously and deliver their results as if nothing is the problem. The lights depend wholly on the battery which in turn relies on a properly functioning alternator.

The alternator depends on a running engine to symbiotically supply it with the electric power needed to fire the plugs. The engine and the lights source their power from the battery that represents a functioning energy reservoir. The car won't function without a battery but it will run without lights.

A good battery assures us of good policies and good sensors will tell you when to pay attention to it. We must ensure that we are focused on keeping the engine running smoothly before we think of the lights.

The battery is the civil service. It keeps the engine and sensors all working and has its usefulness felt everywhere. They are many times apolitically political but they must be fully charged to function well.

Do not allow the lights to get you thinking that they are a euphemism for a whole car. If you keep playing your part and encouraging others to do the same, everyone shall eventually play their part well.

The private sector is the alternator. It ensures that everything — the economy included, is well powered but it needs the engine to function for that is where the market is.

When everyone is allowed to be an unregulated salesman, we cultivate conmen. We cannot all be politicians for we make bad ones if our calling is elsewhere. We will know them by their fruits. If they are not shedding light, then they are something else other than politicians.

Play your role or the car burns down. By the way, lights comprise less than 10% of the car's surface area, why should they occupy 90% of your mind? There are many other things to do, and they must be done very well. As for the politicians, please stop overrating yourselves, your job is kumulika for your constituents and not kufunika. Mhh.

Chapter 8

Why Is The Bee Bigger Than The Elephant?

The male African elephant weighs as much as 14,000 pounds or just over 6,000 kilograms. In contrast, the bee weighs 0.00025 pounds. This means that up to 56 million bees are needed to match the jumbo's weight. A single bee hive has up to 50 thousand bees. This also means that 56 million bees can make 1,120 hives or more. Let us pack this a little.

There is a saying that "the noise of a frog in the river will not stop an elephant from drinking water." This refers to one never allowing things blown out of proportion from distracting their focus. Another one says that "when an elephant is in trouble, even a frog will kick it." This refers to situations where when a strong person is in trouble, be it of a long- or short-term nature, even those they helped out along the way kick them or even want to trip them to fall harder. They pull them down to get ahead of them.

These are sayings but in the African bush, we all fear any swarm of bees because of the lethal impact of their attack on us. A single bee will sting but most times, that won't leave permanent effects on its victim.

That tiny bee is what the elephant fears the most. A single bee humming around it will get it running like it's paid to do so. It has no way of confronting it and a single sting on the vulnerable ears is too painful for it to bear. In fact, communities living in areas visited by elephants, rear bees as a dual-purpose insect. They effectively ward off elephant invasions on their farms whilst the farmers enjoy consuming the honey at no cost at all.

Whenever there is an elephant in the room, meaning that there is a big problem that is difficult to solve, the best way to overcome it is by finding it a bee so that it energetically leaves the room. This is a talent many people wish they could have.

We spend a lot of our time in finding the bee. That is the irony of life. It is the small things that matter the most.

The daily grind is more important than the huge profits we seek to reap. The first step to working out anything in life is of greater importance than the steps ahead when everything is moving like clockwork.

What happens when we have two elephants in the room? Do we find more bees or is one bee just as effective? If the bee is loud enough, both elephants will take off at the same time. This is what happens when we find the antidote for unrelated problems such as when we fail to arrive at a consensus in a meeting and if we don't, we get dissolved as a committee or board. One bee is enough to get those two elephants out of the room. We love the allowances that we currently enjoy at every sitting and the stalemate is not a matter of life and death so it will only take one person vacating their earlier position and joining the guys supporting the lesser evil.

And what if the elephants meet with bees at night? Do they grope in the dark or do they have ready road maps to use at night? In the unlikely event that such a mishap befalls them, it may be a case of "every man for himself and God for us all" but they will have bolted. This is what happens when the best way to solve the problem is via an ambush.

When people illegally occupy private property and proceed to use it as if it belongs to them, the best time to move them out with minimum resistance is in the dead of the night when most are asleep. The authorities will get them out one by one and by morning, everyone will have left the area.

When we are not seeking bees to get elephants out of rooms, they are busy making honey. So, from our 1,120 hives earlier, at an average of 20 kilograms of honey per hive, we can make 22,400 kilograms of honey. And at Kes. 300 a kilo, you make Kes. 6.7 million or more. These are from bees of equivalent weight to one elephant. Do you think that one elephant will fetch you the same amount of money having singly eaten what 15 cows consume? Not unless you are a poacher. I have my doubts and please don't kill them, they deserve to live too. So, all factors kept constant, who is bigger now?